The Last Cow on the White House Lawn and Other Little-Known Facts About the Presidency

Written and illustrated by
BARBARA SEULING

SCHOLASTIC BOOK SERVICES
NEW YORK • TORONTO • LONDON • AUCKLAND • SYDNEY • TOKYO

For Harriet Wasserman,
with love

ISBN 0-590-31313-4

Copyright © 1978 by Barbara Seuling. All rights reserved. This edition is published by Scholastic Book Services, a Division of Scholastic Magazines, Inc., 50 West 44 Street, New York, N.Y. 10036, by arrangement with Doubleday & Company, Inc.

12 11 10 9 8 7 6 5 4 3 2 1   9   0 1 2 3 4 5/8

The Last Cow on the White House Lawn

George Washington (1789–1797)

George Washington held the first presidential barbecue in 1793, when he roasted a 500-pound ox for a party.

During his first year as President of the United States, Washington ran a ferry service across the Potomac.

The famous portrait of Washington painted by Gilbert Stuart was actually finished by another artist, who used John Adams' son-in-law to pose for the unfinished limbs and body.

The United States had a Vice President before it had a President. John Adams was sworn in as Vice President on April 21, 1789, nine days before George Washington was sworn in as the first President, April 30, 1789.

When titles were being discussed, John Adams proposed that George Washington be called "His Highness, the President." Washington, for a while, preferred "His Mightiness the President." Neither was adopted.

George Washington's mother was a constant complainer. One time, she petitioned the Virginia General Assembly for public assistance to prevent her from starving, although her son took very good care of her.

Martha's spelling was so poor that George often had to write letters for her. She spelled "cat" with two t's.

Washington's second inaugural address was the shortest in history, 135 words. The longest was William Henry Harrison's, which ran 8,443 words.

One of George Washington's favorite menus was cream of peanut soup, Smithfield ham with oyster sauce, mashed sweet potatoes with coconut, string beans with mushrooms, southern spoon bread, and Martha's Virginia whiskey cake.

By age fifty-seven, George Washington had lost nearly all of his own teeth. During his endless search for comfortable false teeth, a French dentist made him a set from carved rhinoceros ivory.

John Adams (1797–1801)

John Adams was able to read in seven different languages.

The Adams family was the nation's first First Family to live in the White House.

On his arrival in Washington, John Adams found a swamp and a forest surrounding the President's house. Inside, only six rooms were ready. The principal stairs were not up. There was no bell to summon the servants. It took thirteen fires throughout the mansion just to get rid of some of the dampness. For lack of a better place, Abigail hung her laundry in the empty East Room.

Once, on their way home to the President's house, Abigail and John Adams got lost in the woods of Washington, D.C. They were led out by a passing stranger.

Adams played with his grandson by pulling the little boy around on a kitchen chair. He was the horse.

John Adams was bald.

John Adams took the unpopular stand of acting as lawyer to some British soldiers who were on trial for firing into a threatening Boston mob shortly before the Revolution. He believed that everyone was entitled to a fair trial, no matter what.

When Adams lay dying, he resigned himself to the fact that his rival, Thomas Jefferson, still lived. However, just a few hours earlier on the same day, Jefferson had died. The day was the fiftieth anniversary of the Declaration of Independence, July 4, 1826.

John Adams had the longest life span of any President — nearly ninety-one years.

Thomas Jefferson (1801–1809)

Thomas Jefferson warded off colds by soaking his feet in cold water every morning.

Jefferson wrote his own epitaph. It reads: *Here was buried Thomas Jefferson, author of the Declaration of Independence, of the Statute of Virginia for Religious Freedom, and the father of the University of Virginia.* He never mentioned being President of the United States.

The tradition of the inaugural parade started with Thomas Jefferson, who walked back from the swearing-in ceremony at the Capitol to his boarding house with some people following along behind him.

Jefferson is the President with the most living descendants.

Jefferson's grandson James Madison Randolph was the first baby born in the White House.

Jefferson suffered from migraine headaches.

Jefferson was among the first persons in the nation to be inoculated against smallpox.

President Jefferson kept a pet mockingbird in his study at the White House. It rode on his shoulder or hopped along behind him, and Jefferson taught the bird to take food from his lips.

At his receptions, President Jefferson instituted the handshake, which he felt was more democratic than the bow from the waist.

Thomas Jefferson was an accomplished violinist.

Although he had a French chef, Jefferson loved to cook. He wrote favorite recipes into his cookbook and also wrote an essay called "Observations on Soups." Jefferson introduced ice cream, waffles, and macaroni to the United States.

The White House wine bill during Thomas Jefferson's administration was well over $10,000.

Jefferson imported plants for study and experiment. He was the first President to grow a tomato; at the time, tomatoes were thought to be poisonous. He confessed that, had he been given a choice of position in life, he would have been a gardener.

After the burning of the Library of Congress in the War of 1812, Thomas Jefferson's personal library was bought by the government to start off the rebuilt library.

Jefferson understood Italian, Spanish, French, Irish, Latin, and Greek.

In his collection of fossils, Thomas Jefferson had the jawbone of a mammoth.

Jefferson designed a revolving chair, a pedometer, a revolving music stand, a hemp machine, a portable writing desk, a letter-copying device, and a cannonball-weighted clock that told the day of the week. He had a mechanical device in his wardrobe which revolved to bring his garments to him. The automatic closing doors that are used today on buses are modeled after a design of Jefferson's. But of all his achievements, Thomas Jefferson ranked his authorship of the Declaration of Independence the finest.

James Madison (1809–1817)

James Madison was the first President to wear long trousers.

Friends called Madison by his nickname, "Jemmy."

Glamorous Dolley Madison wore turbans decorated with ostrich feathers and jewels and gave the gayest parties Washington had ever seen. Even after she left the White House, a visit to her house was part of the social whirl of the capital city.

Dolley Madison was seventeen years younger and several inches taller than her husband.

Madison went back to school for postgraduate study after his graduation from Princeton — to study a year of Hebrew.

James Madison wrote nine of the ten amendments that constitute the Bill of Rights.

Mrs. Madison shared with her friends her own special recipe for lipstick.

It is said that when the British arrived at the White House during the burning of Washington in 1814, they found President Madison's dinner on the table and ate it before destroying the mansion.

During President Polk's administration, Dolley Madison, an elderly widow by then, was voted a lifetime seat on the floor of the House by Congress.

James Monroe (1817–1825)

When the Monroes moved into the White House it was practically bare. Monroe sold the government his own furniture, including rare antiques, so that the mansion would be ready for the traditional New Year's reception of 1818.

James Monroe proposed that his cabinet members wear uniforms, but the practice was never adopted.

In 1819 James Monroe became the first President to sail on a steamboat.

Only one foreign country — Liberia — has a capital city named after an American President. The capital is Monrovia, named after James Monroe.

President Monroe was once so upset with his Secretary of the Treasury that he is reported to have driven him out of the White House brandishing a pair of fire tongs.

At a White House dinner President Monroe broke up a fight between the British and the French ministers, who had drawn their swords at each other.

When James Monroe ran for re-election in 1820, he was virtually unopposed. A single dissenting vote was cast on purpose, to be sure that George Washington remained the country's only President elected unanimously.

Monroe was the last President to wear knee breeches, buckled shoes, and three-cornered hats. He adopted the newer fashions long after everyone else had.

John Quincy Adams (1825–1829)

John Quincy Adams was the only President whose father was a President, but he was abroad all the time his father was in office.

All three sons of Louisa and John Quincy Adams — John, George, and Charles Francis — were in love with the same girl. For a while she was engaged to George, then married John. The other two brothers did not attend the wedding. The bride named one of her two children after the two rejected suitors: Georgianna Frances.

John Quincy Adams was a notoriously shabby dresser. Some of his contemporaries swore that he wore the same hat for ten years.

As President, John Quincy Adams rose as early as 4 A.M. to write in his diary. On warm mornings he liked to slip down to the Potomac River behind the White House and skinny-dip. One day a reporter, Anne Royall, surprised him. She sat on his clothes and refused to go away until he promised to give her an interview. She got it.

John Quincy Adams was the only President who was also a published poet.

President John Quincy Adams was a dedicated amateur botanist. He established a botanical garden in Washington, D.C., planted hundreds of trees around the White House. He also grew mulberry trees and his wife, Louisa, spun the silk of the silkworms that lived in them.

Adams is the first President of whom a photograph exists. Born in 1767, he lived long enough to see the camera invented, and toward the end of his life, he had his picture taken.

President Adams loved the game of billiards and bought a billiard table for the White House. The public objected to such a frivolous purchase, and he had to pay for it out of his own pocket.

Andrew Jackson (1829–1837)

Jackson was the only first-generation American to become President. All his forebears were foreign-born.

President Jackson kept a racing stable of thoroughbreds on the White House grounds. He entered them on nearby tracks under other people's names.

Andrew Jackson was the first President in office to ride on a railroad train. John Quincy Adams had taken a ride on a train, but it was after he had left the White House.

Despite his tough reputation, Jackson loved children and had a special relationship with them. He raised eleven in his lifetime, none of them his own.

Andrew Jackson was a notorious brawler. It is believed that he killed several men in his lifetime in various altercations. Some bullets fired in return at him remained in his body. While he was President, one was removed from his right arm from a brawl twenty years earlier. Another was in a bone in his left arm. Still another was lodged next to his heart, and with him all his life.

President Jackson went through four Secretaries of State, five Secretaries of the Treasury, three Secretaries of War, three Secretaries of the Navy, three Attorneys General, and two Postmasters General, in his search for a group with whom he could work satisfactorily.

When Andrew Jackson moved into the White House, he ordered twenty spittoons for the parlors.

Andrew Jackson's favorite dish was turkey hash.

The first attempt to assassinate an American President was made on Andrew Jackson. A deranged man, who believed that Jackson stood in his way of inheriting the British throne, fired two pistols at the President, but neither worked, and Jackson went for him with his walking stick.

When President Jackson left the White House, he had only $90 in his pocket.

Martin Van Buren (1837–1841)

Martin Van Buren wrote an autobiography and never once mentioned his wife, to whom he was married for twelve years.

Van Buren was the first United States President born under the U.S. flag. The seven Presidents before him were born subjects of the British king.

Martin Van Buren drew his entire presidential salary after he completed his term.

Martin Van Buren hired a chef from London to cook his meals at the White House. He dined on the finest china and used gold spoons. To get around town, he rode in an elaborate coach. Some people said that he laced himself up in corsets and scented his whiskers with cologne.

Van Buren discarded the crimson upholstery in the oval drawing room, left over from James Monroe's administration, and changed everything to blue, creating the White House "Blue Room."

William Henry Harrison (1841)

During the presidential campaign of 1840 William Henry Harrison's party, the Whigs, rolled a huge paper ball from Kentucky to the convention in Baltimore, shouting the campaign slogan "Keep the ball rolling to Washington."

Harrison was the only President who ever studied medicine. But he gave it up and became a professional soldier instead.

Neither President Harrison's wife, Anna, nor any of his ten children were present in Washington during his one month in office.

When he first moved into the White House, William Henry Harrison did his own marketing. He even bought a cow and helped the farmer drive it back to the White House through the streets of Washington.

Harrison was President for only thirty-one days and was the first President to die in office. He did not make one single major decision during his term of office. Harrison had caught cold at his inauguration. He developed pneumonia, but actually died of diarrhea while he was being treated.

Since Harrison's death in office in 1841 no President elected in a year ending in a zero has left the White House alive. Some people say that a Shawnee curse put on Harrison at the battle of Tippecanoe, where he got his reputation as an Indian fighter, was responsible.

John Tyler (1841–1845)

John Tyler was found on his hands and knees playing marbles when a messenger brought word that he had succeeded to the presidency. He had to borrow money to get to his inauguration.

No Vice President had succeeded to the presidency on the death of a President before. The Constitution was not clear about whether a Vice President should simply *act* as President in case of a President's death or actually succeed to the presidency. Tyler decided on the latter, setting the precedent for future successions. Some people called Tyler "His Accidency."

The first impeachment proceedings ever to take place against a President were begun against John Tyler in 1843 by those who believed that he had assumed the presidency illegally. The congressional resolution to start the proceedings was not passed.

John Tyler had the most children of any President: fifteen. Eight were by his first wife, Letitia, and seven were by his second wife, Julia. The youngest child, Pearl, was born in 1861, when Tyler was seventy.

Tyler was the first President to marry in office. Tyler's children did not approve of his second marriage and refused to attend the wedding.

John Tyler was an accomplished violinist. Julia, his second wife, played the guitar.

President Tyler's wife Julia had appeared in a New York department store advertisement, which, at the time, was shocking.

Julia Tyler loved dancing and introduced the polka to this country.

Sixteen years after his presidency, John Tyler was elected to the Confederate House of Representatives.

James Knox Polk (1845–1849)

As James Knox Polk spoke at his inauguration, Samuel F. B. Morse sat nearby, tapping out the address on his new invention, the telegraph.

James Polk's family name had originally been "Pollock."

It is said that Polk once had a gallstone operation without anesthesia.

President Polk had no sense of humor. He worked twelve to fourteen hours a day in the White House and hated going out to eat because he might lose half a day's work. He was so exhausted from his four years as President that he died just three months after leaving office.

Strait-laced Sarah Polk believed that serving refreshments at White House receptions was beneath the dignity of the President. Alcoholic beverages were strictly forbidden. At President Polk's Inaugural Ball, music and dancing were stopped short when the presidential couple arrived and were not resumed until after they had left.

During Polk's administration gas lights were installed in the White House. Sarah Polk insisted on leaving one chandelier, illuminated by means of candles, as it was. Her foresight was later praised when, at a White House reception, the new gas lights flickered and failed and the only light remaining was that given off by the candles.

James Knox Polk was the only Speaker of the House to become President.

Polk signed the bill creating the Smithsonian Institution "for the increase and diffusion of knowledge among men."

Zachary Taylor (1849–1850)

Zachary Taylor's legs were so short that he had to be helped up onto his horse.

Taylor did not acknowledge his nomination for the presidency, because he didn't know about it — he had refused to pay the postage due on his formal letter of notification.

For one day, March 4, 1849, David Rice Atchison was President of the United States. Inauguration Day 1849 fell on a Sunday and Zachary Taylor refused to be sworn in on the Sabbath. Therefore, until the following day, March 5, when Taylor took the oath of office, Atchison, President of the Senate and next in line of succession, was technically the President.

President Taylor's old war-horse, Whitey, lived on the White House grounds, where visitors pulled hairs from his tail for souvenirs.

At the time of his nomination, Zachary Taylor had never voted.

Zachary Taylor and James Madison were cousins.

At Taylor's first White House reception six Osage Indians in full regalia were present.

Zachary Taylor died in office after serving only sixteen months of his term. Doctors said that his death was the result of drinking cold milk after eating cherries on a hot day.

Taylor's wife lived in seclusion at the White House. It was rumored that she kept out of sight because she smoked a pipe. At the time of Taylor's death, some people were surprised to learn of her existence.

Millard Fillmore (1850–1853)

One of Millard Fillmore's biggest achievements as President was negotiating a treaty with Peru over the use of guano — bird droppings.

The first bathtub was installed in the White House by President Fillmore, after seeing one at a Cincinnati exhibition in 1850.

The Fillmores bought the first kitchen stove for the White House, but the cook couldn't figure out how it worked. The President visited the Patent Office, read the drawings, saw the model, learned how to work it, and then went back to the White House to teach what he had learned to the cook.

Millard Fillmore's wife Abigail couldn't find a book in the White House when she arrived there as First Lady. She acquired money from Congress and stocked the mansion with books, creating the first White House library.

When Oxford University in England wanted to present Millard Fillmore with an honorary degree, he refused it, feeling that he was not entitled to it.

For some unknown reason, Millard Fillmore's son had all of his father's papers destroyed, leaving a severe gap in American history. President Fillmore has no descendants: both of his children — one son and one daughter — died unmarried.

Franklin Pierce (1853–1857)

Franklin Pierce's running mate, William Rufus De Vane King, took the oath of office in Cuba but never reached Washington. He returned, ill, to his home in Alabama and died there shortly after.

Two months before Franklin Pierce's inauguration, his son Bennie, eleven, was crushed in a train accident in front of his parents, who escaped with minor injuries. The gloom never lifted over the White House for the entire Pierce administration. Mrs. Pierce remained in seclusion for nearly two years and wore black every day, mourning for her dead son and even writing letters to him.

When Franklin Pierce arrived at the White House, the mansion was dark and quiet. No servants answered his call, and he had to make his way to his rooms by candlelight.

President Pierce was arrested for running down an elderly woman while driving his carriage through the streets of Washington. His guilt was not proven and the case was closed.

Franklin Pierce installed the first furnace in the White House, in 1853.

James Buchanan (1857–1861)

James Buchanan was the only bachelor President. He was once engaged, but his fiancee committed suicide after a lovers' quarrel and he never married.

At his home in Wheatland, Pennsylvania, James Buchanan gave sauerkraut-and-mashed-potato parties.

The first inauguration photographed was Buchanan's, in 1857.

Buchanan's niece Harriet Lane, a beautiful blonde with violet eyes, served as White House hostess for her bachelor uncle. She had been brought up by him from the age of nine when she was left an orphan.

Harriet was very popular, much more so than her uncle the President. Songs had been dedicated to her, such as "Listen to the Mockingbird," in 1854.

One of Buchanan's eyes was farsighted and one was nearsighted, and when he talked he tilted his head to one side to adjust his vision.

Abraham Lincoln (1861–1865)

Abraham Lincoln was the first President born outside the borders of the thirteen original states.

Before winning the presidential election of 1860, Lincoln was defeated in eight elections.

Copies of Lincoln's inaugural address of 1861 reached California by Pony Express. It took seventy-five ponies seven days and seventeen hours.

Lincoln's most famous address, the Gettysburg address, was given while he was suffering from smallpox.

Mary Todd Lincoln, the President's wife, was a clothes fanatic; she ran up a $27,000 debt without her husband's knowledge. At the time of the election of 1864 she was terrified that he would lose and find out about her bills.

Abraham Lincoln greatly disliked wearing gloves. Every time his wife, Mary, gave him another pair, he stuffed them into his coat pocket and forgot about them. Once, his pockets bulged from seven pairs.

Abraham Lincoln was the only President to have a patent issued in his name. It was U. S. Patent No. 6,469, for a hydraulic device which could lift ships over shoals.

Lincoln was once challenged to a duel and even got to choose the weapons — cavalry sabers. However, the two men made up and the duel never took place.

To amuse the President's young son Tad, Secretary of War Edwin Stanton conferred a make-believe commission of lieutenant on the boy, complete with uniform and sword. Tad took it very seriously. He dismissed guards, ordered muskets, and armed the gardeners and servants. Once he sentenced a doll named Jack to execution for falling asleep at his sentry post, and the President had to write out a pardon for the doll.

Lincoln appointed the youngest general in American history: Galusha Pennypacker, age twenty.

By a strange quirk of fate, Robert Lincoln, one of the President's sons, was at the scene of three presidential assassinations — his father's in 1865, Garfield's in 1881, and McKinley's in 1901.

Andrew Johnson (1865–1869)

Andrew Johnson never spent a day in school. Fellow workers in a tailor shop taught him the alphabet, he taught himself to read, and his girl friend taught him to write.

When he ran away as an apprentice tailor, Andrew Johnson met a girl who became his friend. He helped her make a quilt before he went on his way.

In later life, even during his political career, Johnson was proud of his skill as a tailor. When he was governor of Tennessee, he made a suit for the governor of Kentucky.

Johnson was the first President to become a U.S. Senator after leaving the White House as President.

Ulysses S. Grant (1869–1877)

The salary of the President doubled, from $25,000 to $50,000, during Grant's administration.

Grant was christened Hiram Ulysses Grant. The initials of this choice — H.U.G. — always bothered him. Later, at West Point, when he was mistakenly entered as "Ulysses Simpson Grant," he left his name that way.

President Grant, a great Civil War hero, got queasy at the sight of a piece of rare meat.

A favorite breakfast of Grant's during the Civil War was a cucumber soaked in vinegar.

The coldest Inauguration Day was in 1873, when Ulysses S. Grant was sworn in as President for the second time. The temperature was 4°F. In the outdoor pavilions the champagne was frozen solid and the guests danced in overcoats. Hundreds of imported canaries sat on their perches, unable to utter a peep.

President Grant was arrested in Washington for speeding in his horse and carriage. The arresting officer was about to let him go when he recognized the President, but Grant insisted he do his duty and later commended him for it.

Grant was the first President of the United States to entertain a reigning monarch, when King Kalakaua of the Sandwich Islands (Hawaii) visited. At a state dinner in the White House, the King's servants examined every bit of food before passing it on to their King.

President Grant established the first National Park, Yellowstone, during his administration.

Ulysses S. Grant smoked twenty cigars a day.

At the White House stable in 1864, Grant's chief groom, Albert, talked and ate with the animals.

Mrs. Grant was about to have an operation to uncross her eyes when the President convinced her that her eyes were fine, crossed and all.

President Grant's daughter, Nellie, was born on the Fourth of July. She grew up thinking that the fireworks on that day were for her birthday.

Nellie Grant had one of the most lavish weddings ever held in the White House. The wedding breakfast consisted of soft-shelled crab, chicken croquettes, lamb cutlets, beef tongue in aspic, woodcock and snipe on toast, salad, seven kinds of dessert, and three beverages. There were twelve bridesmaids in identical gowns at the wedding, and even the bridegroom carried a bouquet of flowers. Among $75,000-worth of wedding gifts was a poem written by Walt Whitman to the bride.

Jesse Grant, the President's son, was an enterprising stamp collector. He persuaded American ambassadors abroad to send him foreign stamps. When his mother insisted that he write thank-you notes for stamps received, Jesse abandoned his plan.

Jesse ordered stamps from a bargain outfit that never came. He sent a letter to the outfit, with the help of his policeman friend, Kelly, saying, "I am a Capitol policeman. I can arrest anybody, anywhere, at any time, for anything. I want you to send those stamps to Jesse Grant." It was signed, "Kelly, Capitol policeman." The stamps arrived shortly after.

Rutherford B. Hayes
(1877–1881)

On the eve of Rutherford Hayes's inauguration the controversial election of 1876 was still under investigation. Mr. and Mrs. Hayes left for Washington not knowing whether or not they were the First Family. En route they received word that he had officially been declared elected.

President Hayes's wife, Lucy, served no liquor in the White House and became known as "Lemonade Lucy." At the White House wedding of the President's niece Emily Platt, the bride was toasted in tea, coffee, and lemonade.

Mrs. Hayes was the first President's wife who was a college graduate.

President Hayes removed several men from government service because he felt they were using their positions to further their own causes. One of these men was Chester Arthur, a future President.

The Hayes family frequently had overnight guests. If all the beds and couches were used, son Webb Hayes had to sleep in the White House attic on an old unused billiard table.

Sometimes, with all the guests milling about, President Hayes had to lock himself in a bathroom to concentrate on his work.

During the Hayes administration, the first telephone was installed in the White House. The President talked to Alexander Graham Bell over thirteen miles of wire. His first words into the new machine were "Please speak a little more slowly."

The Hayeses celebrated their silver wedding anniversary in the White House. At the ceremony, they were married again by the same preacher who had originally married them. Mrs. Hayes wore her original wedding gown.

Hayes was the first President to visit the West Coast, in 1880.

Mrs. Hayes hand-painted her own china. Some of it was quite unappetizing, representing animals fighting and birds eating rotting vegetables.

First Lady Lucy Hayes introduced the practice of egg-rolling on the White House lawn at Easter time.

James A. Garfield (1881)

James Garfield could write with both hands at the same time. Sometimes he wrote Greek with one hand and Latin with the other.

During the Civil War, Garfield, who was a colonel in the Union Army, studied training manuals, historical battles, and models which he constructed himself and plotted battles, using wooden blocks for soldiers.

James Garfield may have foreseen his own death. Only a couple of days before he was shot, he sent for Robert Lincoln, the only surviving son of Abraham Lincoln, and went over every detail of his father's assassination. And only months before his own death, Garfield had taken out an insurance policy for $25,000.

The public, concerned after the President's death about the welfare of his family, raised over $300,000 for Mrs. Garfield and the children.

The undertaker who arranged President Garfield's funeral claimed that in all the confusion, he never got paid.

Chester A. Arthur (1881–1885)

When Chester Alan Arthur, Garfield's Vice President, suddenly became President, he refused to move into the White House until it had been thoroughly cleaned out of all junk and refurnished to his satisfaction. Twenty-four wagonloads of rugs, furniture, and other White House belongings were carted off and sold at public auction for about $3,000.

Chester Arthur wore mourning for the assassinated President Garfield for six months.

Shaken by the death of his predecessor, Arthur composed a document before he left his New York home for Washington, proclaiming that should he die, the Senate should elect a President pro tempore, or temporary President, so that the nation's business could go on uninterrupted.

A man of fashion, Chester Arthur was the first President to have a valet. It was rumored that he had eighty pairs of trousers and ordered twenty-five new coats at one time. When Arthur fell out of favor, some people said that he was "defeated by his trousers."

Chester Arthur personally supported the first Civil Service Act, which made it necessary to pass tests to get certain government jobs. It had been a disappointed office-seeker who had shot President Garfield.

Arthur had a French chef in the White House. Dinners often lasted two or three hours.

Arthur's personal floral bill for one state dinner was $1,500. Although flowers were grown in the White House conservatory, he still ordered large amounts from New York.

President Arthur always had a flower in his buttonhole and a silk handkerchief in his vest pocket. At White House receptions, he wore white gloves. "Elegant Arthur," whose complexion was once described as being like strawberries and cream, drove around Washington in a dark green landau drawn by mahogany bays, his lap covered with monogrammed blankets.

President Arthur never permitted his children to be photographed or interviewed.

Arthur was fond of sleigh rides down Pennsylvania Avenue.

Chester Arthur was considered one of the finest fishermen in America. He once caught an eighty-pound bass off the coast of Rhode Island.

Arthur's Secretary of War was Abraham Lincoln's son, Robert.

The Arthur administration enacted the first major immigration law, which excluded paupers, criminals, idiots, and the insane.

Chester Arthur had one of the shortest life spans of all the Presidents, excluding those who were assassinated. He died of Bright's disease at age fifty-six.

Grover Cleveland
(1885–1889, 1893–1897)

Grover Cleveland was the only President to serve two separate terms. He left the White House in 1889 and returned four years later for a second term.

Cleveland was the first President to use fireworks at his inauguration.

Within a span of only three and a half years, Grover Cleveland had been mayor of Buffalo, New York, governor of New York State, and President of the United States.

As sheriff of Erie County, in Buffalo, New York, Cleveland had sprung the trap at two executions, making him the only President who was once a hangman.

Cleveland was the only President married in the White House. He wrote out the invitations himself and in the wedding ceremony had the word "obey" deleted from the bride's vows.

President Cleveland had known his young wife from the day she was born and bought her her first baby carriage. Her father had been Cleveland's law partner.

On the day of his wedding, President Cleveland worked in his office until 7 P.M. before getting ready for the ceremony and party.

Frances Cleveland loved birds, and the White House was filled with them. The President could not concentrate one night because of the singing of one pet mockingbird, which finally had to be banished to another part of the mansion.

Mrs. Cleveland was the first wife of a President to give birth to a child in the White House. The baby was Esther Cleveland.

The President's baby daughter Ruth was taken for outings on the White House lawn until visitors started picking her up and passing her around. Afterward the White House gates were closed to the public, and rumors began that the child was being hidden away because of a deformity.

The candy bar "Baby Ruth" was named after the little daughter of President Cleveland.

Grover Cleveland's favorite dish was corned beef and cabbage.

Cleveland wrote all his own letters in longhand.

President Cleveland relaxed by fishing or hunting. He had a shotgun named "Death and Destruction."

Grover Cleveland underwent a secret operation when he was President of the United States, which wasn't revealed until twenty-five years after it took place, because Cleveland did not want to throw the country into a panic over his health. His entire upper left jaw had to be removed because of a cancerous growth on the roof of his mouth. The operation was performed on board a yacht. Later, an artificial jaw was made to conceal the problem.

Benjamin Harrison (1889–1893)

Benjamin Harrison's grandfather was also a President — William Henry Harrison.

When eleven members of the Benjamin Harrison family moved into the White House in 1889, there was one bathroom in the entire mansion.

During Benjamin Harrison's stay in the White House, a professional ratcatcher had to be hired for the mansion.

Congress gave the Harrisons money to do over the White House and install electric lights for the first time. When floors and walls were removed for the renovation, Mrs. Harrison found old cupboards and shelves with pieces of china and crystal from former administrations. With those pieces she started the White House china collection.

For exercise, President Harrison used a rowing machine, which he bought for $36.

"Baby" McKee, the President's grandchild, was a favorite subject of press photographers. One day the goat, His Whiskers, ran off with Baby McKee in a cart behind him, and the President, in his tall silk hat and frock coat, ran after them.

When electricity was installed in the White House during Benjamin Harrison's administration, the President's family went to bed at night leaving all the lights burning. Everyone was afraid to touch the switches.

President Harrison started the custom of flying the United States flag from public buildings.

Harrison made one hundred forty speeches in thirty days during a tour and never repeated a single speech.

John Scott Harrison, a farmer born in Indiana, was both the son and the father of a President. William Henry Harrison was his father and Benjamin Harrison was his son.

Benjamin Harrison and his second wife had a baby daughter a year after his son, Russell, at age forty-three, had had a son.

William McKinley (1897–1901)

As a soldier in the Civil War, eighteen-year-old William McKinley, serving under another future President, Rutherford B. Hayes, drove a coffee wagon to the men on the battlefields.

There was an elevator in the McKinley White House but it operated by water pressure from a tank on the roof, and the pressure was usually too low to move it.

Ida Saxton McKinley, the President's wife, suffered from seizures and could pass out in the middle of a conversation without falling from her chair. When this happened, the President simply threw a handkerchief over her face until she came to and continued the conversation.

William McKinley was the last Civil War veteran to become President.

While governor of Ohio, McKinley got stuck with a debt of $130,000, through notes he had endorsed for someone as a favor. Friends helped him to raise funds so that he could continue his political career, but as President each pay check was turned over to a treasurer of a special fund to repay the debt. The money was invested wisely, the debt paid, and an estate of $200,000 was built up for the President.

McKinley loved cigars, but wouldn't be photographed with one. He didn't want to set a bad example for the children of America.

Ida McKinley hated the color yellow. On the White House lawn in spring, the grounds were covered with flowers — with not a single yellow one among them.

William McKinley always wore a lucky red carnation in his lapel. At an exposition in Buffalo, New York, after he had given his flower to a little girl in the crowd, he was shot by an assassin. He died eight days later from the wounds.

Theodore Roosevelt
(1901–1909)

Theodore Roosevelt, McKinley's Vice President, was the youngest man to become President. He was forty-two when he succeeded to the presidency.

Roosevelt loved sweet potatoes so much that he had some shipped from his home on Long Island to the White House.

Theodore Roosevelt established the first White House press room after he found several reporters shivering outside the gate one day.

Teddy Roosevelt spent several years as a cowboy in the Dakota Badlands. When a gunslinger looked at his eyeglasses and called him "Four Eyes," Roosevelt knocked him down and took away his gun.

Every member of Roosevelt's family had a pair of wooden stilts.

First Lady Ethel Roosevelt was so good at sports that Quentin once said, "I'll bet Mother was a boy when she was little."

Big-game-hunter Teddy Roosevelt had the heads of the animals he bagged stuffed and mounted on the White House walls. Later, when First Lady Eleanor Roosevelt remembered her early visits to the White House to visit her Uncle Teddy, she reported how disconcerting it was to eat one's dinner with all those eyes looking down upon the table.

Roosevelt kept a rhinoceros-foot inkwell on his desk in the White House.

Theodore Roosevelt's son Quentin recruited his classmates into "the White House Gang." Once, the boys dropped a giant snowball off the White House portico onto a policeman. Another time they threw spitballs at the portrait of Andrew Jackson in the White House corridor. Always, when the boys were caught in mischief, the President lectured them severely.

A friend asked Teddy Roosevelt why he did not make his daughter Alice behave. He said that he could run the country or control Alice, but not both.

Theodore Roosevelt set the record for presidential handshaking. On New Year's Day 1907 he shook hands with 8,513 people.

President Roosevelt's daughter Ethel is said to have been the greatest tomboy who ever lived in the White House. Tobogganing down the White House stairs on cookie sheets was one of her favorite pastimes.

Roosevelt joined his children at play whenever he could find the time. After some strenuous racing about the attic, he once sat down on a slip-covered chair for a breath. Suddenly, the chair collapsed beneath him. It had actually been two of the boys with a cloth draped over them, pretending to be a chair.

At daughter Alice's lavish wedding at the White House, the knife given her to cut her wedding cake was too small, so she borrowed the sword of a presidential aide and slashed through the cake with vigor.

Roosevelt had once refused to shoot a bear cub while hunting, which inspired a political cartoon. The bear in the cartoon further inspired toy manufacturers, and the result was the "Teddy Bear." It is still a favorite toy of children.

Teddy Roosevelt kept one of the most rigorous daily routines of any President. As a child, he had been sick so much that he had to be taught at home instead of sent off to school. His father had built him a gymnasium outside the window of his room, where the boy strengthened his body and became a robust and healthy teen-ager. For the rest of his life, he kept fit and trim in any active way that he could. As President, he did violent daily exercises. He had bouts in the East Room with Japanese jujitsu experts and Chinese wrestlers. He walked vigorously, challenging Secret Service men to keep up with him as he crossed streams, cut through underbrush, and climbed hills. He boxed with a trainer named Sixsmith, played tennis, and rode horseback daily.

One day TR had a friendly boxing match with a young naval officer. The President received a blow on his left eye, which ruptured a blood vessel. A physician warned him to cut down on strenuous activity if he wanted to save the eye, but TR continued his vigorous activities; by 1908, four years after the boxing incident, Roosevelt had lost the sight of his left eye completely. The secret was kept for years, so that the feelings of the young officer would be spared.

Theodore Roosevelt could read three books in a single evening.

In 1912, during a campaign for a second presidency, Theodore Roosevelt was shot in an attempted assassination. The bullet lodged in his chest, but Roosevelt went on with his speech and afterward went to a hospital, where the bullet was removed. A metal eyeglass case in his breast pocket had stopped it from going through to his heart, and he recovered quickly from the wound.

The Smithsonian Institution in Washington has the typed campaign speech which was also in Teddy Roosevelt's pocket at the time of the shooting — with the bullet hole in it.

William Howard Taft
(1909–1913)

President William Howard Taft had a reputation for falling asleep in conferences, while signing papers, sitting for his portrait — anywhere. Once he fell asleep at a funeral.

Taft weighed over three hundred pounds. Once he got stuck in the White House bathtub and had to be helped out. A special bathtub, big enough for four average men, had to be built for him.

Expecting his father's inauguration address to be boring, young Charlie Taft brought along *Treasure Island* to read.

President Taft started the tradition of the President throwing out the first ball of the opening of the baseball season. He loved the sport, and the White House had his box at the ball park equipped with a special oversize chair to accommodate his bulk.

Taft was the first President to have government automobiles at his disposal. He had a fleet of four cars — a White Steamer, two Pierce-Arrows, and a Baker Electric.

Either Mrs. Taft or the President's physician always had the President on one diet or another, which made him irritable. When he went off on a train trip and discovered that Mrs. T. had the dining car of the train removed, he was furious. He ordered that the train stop at the next station and a dining car be attached. "What's the use of being President," he cried, "if you can't have a train with a diner on it?"

After Helen, his wife, suffered a stroke in 1909, President Taft taught her to speak again.

Taft was the last President to keep a cow on the White House lawn. The cow was Pauline Wayne, a Holstein. She lived in the garage, among the President's automobiles, and supplied the milk that was served at the White House table.

Once President Taft got caught picking flowers in front of the Department of Agriculture and was about to be arrested when the watchman recognized him and let him go.

William Howard Taft was the first President whose salary was subject to federal income tax.

President Taft's wife, Helen, is the person responsible for all the cherry trees planted in the city of Washington. After she made a trip to Japan, the mayor of Tokyo sent her a gift of three thousand trees. She planted the first one herself. Today the cherry blossoms are a noted tourist attraction in springtime Washington.

William Howard Taft was the only person to hold the two highest offices in the nation, President and Chief Justice of the United States Supreme Court.

Woodrow Wilson (1913–1921)

President Wilson typed his own letters. His typewriter could be adapted to type in either English or Greek.

Woodrow Wilson was the first President with a Ph.D. degree, but in his heart he wished he had been a vaudeville actor.

Wilson was superstitious about the number 13. It was the number of letters in his name and the number of the original American colonies. Arriving in France after World War I for a peace conference, the President had the ship slow down to arrive on the thirteenth.

Woodrow Wilson thought inaugural balls were frivolous and didn't have one.

Wilson and his first wife, Ellen, exchanged more than a thousand love notes in their twenty-nine years of marriage.

Daughter Margaret Wilson, a voice student and aspiring concert singer, lost her singing voice touring army camps and giving concerts during World War I.

Edith Wilson, the President's second wife, learned to ride a bicycle along the corridors of the White House.

Margaret used to lead her younger sisters out of the White House wearing disguises and went

on sight-seeing tours of Washington, including the White House.

Because of the manpower shortage during World War I, the Wilsons kept a flock of sheep on the White House lawn to keep the grass trimmed. The wool from the shearing was sold and the money sent to the Red Cross. Among the sheep was a ram named Old Ike, who chewed tobacco.

Woodrow Wilson became one of the most ardent golfers ever to live in the White House. He was first introduced to the game by the family physician, to help him get over his first wife's death. He later played every day before breakfast, and when the White House lawn was covered with snow, he would paint the balls black so they would show up.

As part of the war effort in World War I, there were such things as "meatless" days and "wheatless" days. On "gasless Sundays" the Wilsons went to church in a horsedrawn carriage.

Woodrow Wilson liked to do imitations of Teddy Roosevelt. He also danced the jig and told jokes.

Wilson could not read properly until he was nine years old. Until then, he read everything backward.

Wilson's second wife, Edith, was a descendant of the Indian princess Pocahontas.

When President Wilson suffered a stroke Mrs. Wilson would not let anyone see him without first getting her approval. She decided whom the President should see and which papers he should sign. Some people said she ran the country and called her "Presidentress." She was the only person who knew the secret code by which the President communicated with emissaries in Europe.

During his illness, which lasted about a year and a half, four hundred movies were shown in the White House for the ailing President.

Warren G. Harding (1921–1923)

Warren G. Harding was the first President for whom women could vote.

To get in shape for his presidential campaign, Harding played Ping-Pong every morning, tennis every afternoon, and golf a couple of times each week.

Harding was the first person to ride to his inauguration in an automobile.

At nineteen Warren G. Harding ran a newspaper in Marion, Ohio. After his inauguration he went back to Marion and stopped at his old newspaper office, rolled up his sleeves, and helped make up the paper. As President, he carried a printer's rule in his vest pocket as a good luck charm.

Harding was the first President to use a radio. One was installed in the White House on February 8, 1922.

Laddie Boy, Harding's Airedale, owned Washington Dog License Number 1. Every day he delivered the President's newspapers. At the White House, Laddie Boy had his own valet.

President Harding saved a dog's life by executive clemency. The dog had been brought into the country illegally and was ordered put to death by a Pennsylvania judge. The President wrote a personal plea on behalf of the dog and the governor of Pennsylvania pardoned him.

Harding introduced toothpicks to the White House.

Laddie Boy had a birthday party at which a cake was served made of many layers of dog biscuits topped with icing.

The first salmon of the season was sent, traditionally, to the President. News photographers showed up at the White House to see the one sent to President Harding and found that the cook had cut off the salmon's head so that he could fit the fish into the ice box. An ingenious soul produced a needle and thread, the head was sewn back on, the fish was photographed, and nobody knew the difference.

Mrs. Warren G. Harding, a cold and imperious woman, was called "The Duchess" by the President and his friends.

President Harding kept a pen of turkeys at the White House.

When President Harding died, the Newsboys' Association began a movement to have a statue made of his dog, Laddie Boy, as a tribute to the President. Every newsboy in America was asked to contribute a penny of their earnings for it. The statue now stands in the Smithsonian Institution.

Calvin Coolidge (1923–1929)

Calvin Coolidge played the harmonica, could sew a quilt, had an American Indian ancestor, and could doctor a sick maple tree. When he came to live in the White House, he brought his rocking chair with him. After dinner, he sat out on the front porch of the White House. He had to give it up, however, when crowds started to gather to watch him rock.

Sometimes Coolidge tried to sneak past the Secret Service guards to take a walk by himself, but no matter which door he tried, a guard was covering it. He was never able to elude them.

President Coolidge sometimes wandered about the White House in his nightshirt.

Coolidge was known for snooping. Sometimes he went down to the mailroom to look through the letters himself. Often he was found in the kitchen or pantry; it irritated him that he could never figure out what happened to leftovers at the White House. One day a Library of Congress staff member went over to the Executive mansion to arrange the books in the library. The President's dog kept bothering him, until finally he threw a book at it. The

61

book hit something hard behind a curtain and bounced off. Out stepped the President. "Warm, isn't it?" he said.

When the news came that President Harding was dead, Vice President Coolidge was sworn

in by his father, a notary, in the light of a kerosene lamp, at 2:45 in the morning, at his Vermont farm.

On his first day in the White House, Calvin Coolidge was so lonely that he called the same friend in Boston five times. When he got bored, he pressed all the buttons on the White House desk at once and watched with glee as everyone came running.

President Coolidge, whose first cabinet meeting lasted fifteen minutes, had a reputation for never wasting a penny or a word. At a dinner party, he sat next to a woman who bet him that she could get him to say at least three words. "You lose," he replied.

Guests at the Coolidge White House were served plain ice water in paper cups.

"Coolidge breakfasts" were instituted at the White House as soon as the thrifty President had made sure that the government was authorized to pay for "official" meals. Members of Congress were then invited to these early meals, and the President didn't have to pay for them out of his own pocket.

In another effort to economize, Coolidge tried to raise chickens in the White House yard, but they tasted funny. It turned out that the chickens were being raised right over Teddy Roosevelt's old mint garden.

One White House cook quit because the President was so cheap. The last straw was when he could not be convinced that it took six hams to feed sixty people at a state dinner.

Despite his stinginess, Calvin Coolidge put up more guests at the White House than any other President. One guest, screen cowboy Tom Mix, even brought his horse.

President Coolidge loved animals. Among his many pets were a raccoon that he walked on a leash and a dog named Paul Pry, who was sent to Marine training school to learn some discipline but was sent home because he flunked the course.

When his cat, Tiger, was missing, the President asked local radio stations to broadcast a "missing cat" bulletin, giving a description of Tiger and an appeal for his return. The cat was found, but ran away again and never returned.

The Coolidge daily routine was quite leisurely, with breakfast at 8, work at 9, lunch at 12:30, back to work at 2:30, and quitting time in mid-afternoon. Each afternoon there was a two- or three-hour nap, and bedtime was at 10 P.M.

The President relaxed by riding a mechanical bucking horse which bounced him up and down. When he went fishing, he had a Secret Service man bait his hook.

When Howard Chandler Christy was painting First Lady Grace Coolidge's portrait, the artist asked her to wear a red dress, to contrast with her white collie, Prudence Prim, who would be in the portrait with her. The President objected. "If it's contrast you want," he argued, "why not wear white and paint the dog red?"

Herbert Hoover (1929–1933)

Herbert Hoover was the first President born west of the Mississippi.

Hoover's wife, Lou, spoke four languages fluently and could work in an additional two. Also an expert on metals, she collaborated with her husband, who was a mining engineer, on a translation of an ancient treatise on metals.

During his four years in the White House, Herbert Hoover never attended the theater, nor did he take a vacation after the Depression deepened, until the very end of his term of office when he knew that he had not been re-elected.

Lou Hoover called the President "Bert." He called her "Mother."

Even when dining alone, the Hoovers had seven-course meals.

Herbert Hoover had honorary degrees from over fifty American universities.

President Hoover never accepted his salary as President and spent his own money on entertaining.

For exercise, President Hoover tossed a medicine ball around with members of his cabinet. He was also an excellent fisherman.

"The Star-Spangled Banner" became the official United States national anthem under Herbert Hoover, in 1931.

President Hoover's son Allan had two pet alligators, which sometimes wandered loose around the White House. Another son, Herbert Hoover, Jr., was an inventor who received patents for his oil-locating devices.

Herbert Hoover died at the age of ninety, while working on a book.

Franklin D. Roosevelt
(1933–1945)

When Franklin Roosevelt was five years old, his father took him to the White House to visit the President, Grover Cleveland. Cleveland said to him, "I wish for you that you may never be President."

Franklin Roosevelt was such a popular President that the White House staff measured his mail by the yard.

In Miami, less than a month before his inauguration, Roosevelt missed being assassinated by inches. In the attempt, Mayor Cermak of Chicago, who was sitting next to him, was fatally wounded.

On his arrival at the White House, Roosevelt had John Adams' prayer carved in ivory on the mantel of the fireplace in the White House State Dining Room. It read: "May none but honest and wise men ever rule under this roof."

For his entire presidency — twelve years and thirty-nine days — Franklin Delano Roosevelt could not walk a step without the aid of braces and crutches. He had been paralyzed from the waist down as a result of polio since 1921.

Although his legs were paralyzed, Roosevelt traveled more than any other Chief Executive and at home, wrestled with his sons, two at a time. He also swam, did rigorous exercises, and got around his home either by crawling on his hands from room to room or on his own home-made wheel chair made from a kitchen chair without arms so that he could get on and off by himself.

On their radio shows, Eddie Cantor and the Lone Ranger asked children to send their dimes to President Roosevelt, chairman of the March of Dimes, an annual drive sponsored by the National Foundation for Infantile Paralysis. A hundred thousand dimes a day poured into the White House mail room. Some of them were baked in cakes; others were embedded in wax. Some were taped down. One woman sent in her hair which she asked be sold for dimes for the campaign. Fifty extra postal clerks had to be hired to dig the coins out of other mail. A total of nearly three million dimes were received.

In 1939, FDR became the first President to appear on TV, at the opening of the New York World's Fair, and those who had TV sets watched on 5½-inch screens.

Roosevelt's favorite writer was Mark Twain.

FDR took his Scotch terrier, Fala, everywhere with him. Once, aboard a ship, a crew member snipped off a souvenir lock of the dog's hair.

Other sailors did the same thing and soon Fala had a bald spot. The President was furious.

FDR was the first President to fly in an airplane while in office.

When the King and Queen of England paid a visit to Roosevelt at his Hyde Park, New York, home, he served them hot dogs.

Especially during World War II, food gifts to President Roosevelt had to be analyzed by the Department of Agriculture's laboratory before being presented to him. It paid off once: a fish sent from Cuba was found to have poison in it.

Fala was nicknamed "The Informer" by the Secret Service men guarding President Roosevelt. When the President's travel plans were kept secret during the war years, Fala often gave away the fact that the President was passing through town by insisting on going for a walk at every train stop. People who saw Fala knew that his master was not far away.

Kitchen help at the White House claim that Franklin Roosevelt could get more off the carcass of a turkey than anyone.

Franklin D. Roosevelt appointed the first woman cabinet officer, Frances Perkins, Secretary of Labor. When asked if being a woman was a handicap, Miss Perkins replied, "Only in climbing trees."

Roosevelt loved playing poker, especially with lots of wild cards.

FDR was superstitious. He never left for a trip on a Friday, and he always refused to be third on a match.

Roosevelt was the most avid collector of stamps to inhabit the White House. He took at least one album with him on every trip he made.

Sarah Delano Roosevelt, the President's mother, was the first woman to cast a vote for her son for President of the United States.

In 1905 Franklin Delano Roosevelt married his fifth cousin Eleanor Roosevelt. At the wedding, the President of the United States, Theodore Roosevelt, Eleanor's uncle, gave away the bride.

First Lady Eleanor Roosevelt once appeared at a news conference in a riding habit. She rode over Boulder Dam in a bucket. She started a group for women only, in answer to all-stag dinners which the President and his cabinet officers had. On her way to the Chicago Democratic National Convention in 1940, the pilot let Eleanor Roosevelt fly the plane.

FDR often scrambled eggs for his friends; it was his favorite dish.

Eleanor Roosevelt drove her own car and refused Secret Service protection. As a compromise, she had to keep a pistol in the glove compartment.

During the Roosevelt administration the first electric dishwasher and the first bomb shelter were installed in the White House.

Franklin Delano Roosevelt designed American eagle pedestals for the grand piano in the White House East Room.

The Cabinet Room created during FDR's administration had originally been a clothes-drying yard.

Mrs. Roosevelt had to make formal appointments with the President if the children had to see him about something important.

At the first inauguration of Franklin Delano Roosevelt, the President had two grandchildren. When he was inaugurated the second time, he had thirteen.

Harry S Truman (1945–1953)

Harry Truman's full middle name was "S" — with no period after it.

During the Truman administration, the White House began to collapse around the First Family. Daughter Margaret's sitting room was sinking, the chandelier in the East Room trembled overhead as the President received guests, and the whole floor of his study swayed. Renovations were ordered, and the First Family went to live in Blair House, normally used for State guests. They remained there from 1948 to 1952.

Harry Truman was the only twentieth-century President who never attended college.

When Harry Truman was sworn in as President of the United States, he was so nervous that he had to read the oath of office from a slip of paper.

Truman's father was known as "Peanuts" Truman.

By age fourteen Harry S Truman had read every book in the Independence, Missouri, public library.

As a boy, Truman got up at 5 A.M. to practice the piano for two hours before school started.

During his boyhood in Missouri, Harry Truman's family saved up its dimes and threw them into the tray of an old trunk. When enough had accumulated, his father would send away for books. The family acquired a whole set of Shakespeare this way.

After the White House renovation was completed, President Truman conducted the first White House tour himself.

Harry Truman met his future wife, Bess, when she was six years old. He said she was the only girl in Independence who could whistle through her teeth.

Margaret Truman refused to become engaged while she lived in the White House, because, she said, she couldn't be sure if she was liked for herself or for her position.

One of Harry Truman's hobbies was architecture. As a county judge in Missouri, he had been in charge of building two courthouses.

President Truman had official White House cars designed to accommodate the top hats which the President sometimes had to wear.

Medicare identification card No. 1 was issued in 1966 to former President Harry S Truman. Card No. 2 was issued to Bess, his wife.

On his eighty-seventh birthday, former President Truman refused the House of Representatives' offer to bestow on him the Congressional Medal of Honor. He felt he had done nothing to deserve it.

Dwight D. Eisenhower
(1953–1961)

President Dwight D. Eisenhower was the first President to appear on color TV.

Eisenhower was the oldest man to serve as President of the United States. He became the only Chief Executive to celebrate his seventieth birthday in the White House.

Ike, as he was called by his friends and admirers, liked to cook, so he had a kitchen put in on the third floor of the White House, in the family quarters.

Later to become a five-star general and President of the United States, Eisenhower had only a fair academic record at West Point. His interest was mainly in football, until, as halfback, he wrenched his knee tackling the great Jim Thorpe, ending his football career.

Eisenhower was the first President to go underwater in an atomic submarine, the U.S.S. *Seawolf*.

President Eisenhower used the White House Blue Room for his hobby of painting. Although he liked to paint, he couldn't draw, so someone had to sketch the pictures for him to paint, resulting in a paint-by-numbers fad around the country.

Dwight D. Eisenhower was the only President to hold a pilot's license. He introduced helicopters to the White House for short presidential trips.

Dwight and Mamie Eisenhower were real TV fans. They liked nothing better than to eat TV dinners on trays and watch Westerns.

The bubbletop limousine for presidential parades was designed by President Eisenhower, but it wasn't ready for his inauguration.

When he was in the hospital recuperating from a heart attack, President Eisenhower received a gag gift from some reporters of a pair of pajamas with five gold stars embroidered on the collar tabs. Good-naturedly, he wore them.

Ike's favorite dessert was prune whip.

In his retirement, Dwight D. Eisenhower scored a hole-in-one while playing golf in Palm Springs, California.

John F. Kennedy (1961–1963)

John F. Kennedy was the only President born under the sign of Gemini. His birthday was May 29.

Kennedy was the youngest man ever elected President. Theodore Roosevelt was a few months younger when he took office, but it was by succeeding a President who had died in office, not by election.

The Kennedy family had many pets, including dogs, a cat, three birds, a horse, three ponies, two hamsters, and a rabbit — John F. Kennedy was allergic to animal fur.

As a boy, John Kennedy, called Jack, had scarlet fever, appendicitis, and diphtheria. In college he suffered an attack of jaundice and injured his back in football practice. During World War II his back injury got worse, and he also suffered from malaria. In 1954, after critical back surgery, Kennedy was so ill that he was given the last rites. Later, as President, he was known for his vigor and for his physical fitness programs.

John F. Kennedy, the first Roman Catholic President, had trouble finding a priest who could hear his confession without recognizing his voice.

During his recuperation from back surgery in 1954, Kennedy wrote the book *Profiles in Courage*, which was published in 1956, became a best-seller, and won a Pulitzer Prize.

Kennedy was the first President born in the twentieth century. His wife, Jacqueline, was the first First Lady born in the twentieth century.

Kennedy's wife had been the "Inquiring Camera Girl" for a Washington newspaper. When daughter Caroline grew up, she got a job as copyperson with the New York *Daily News*.

The Kennedys hated TV and had all the TV sets removed from the White House. But when Caroline cried to see "Lassie," they had to bring one set back.

When President Kennedy went to a restaurant, or took a cab, someone else with him always had to pay; he never carried any cash.

When Kennedy was President, he called his father on the telephone every day.

Kennedy loved *fettucini*, an Italian noodle dish, and movies, especially Westerns and Civil War pictures.

Kennedy could read two thousand words a minute with almost total comprehension.

Lyndon B. Johnson (1963–1969)

In his first-grade class, Lyndon B. Johnson was already boasting that he would one day be the President of the United States.

Johnson was the second tallest President, at six feet three inches. Lincoln was taller by only one inch.

The initials "LBJ" stood for the entire Johnson family: Lyndon Baines Johnson; his wife, Lady Bird Johnson; and his daughters, Lynda Bird Johnson and Luci Baines Johnson. The President said it was cheaper that way when it came to monogramming.

President Johnson had a Texas barbecue on the roof of the White House. He served sizzling steaks, baked potatoes, corn pudding, and pecan pie.

Johnson had a telephone on the dining room table.

Lyndon Johnson was an excellent dancer. Once he waltzed fifty guests in turn around the East Room. Daughter Luci, a teen-ager, taught her father the frug and the watusi.

President Johnson fired one Secret Service agent thirteen times.

Sometimes the President called the press on a moment's notice and had them run along trying to keep up with his brisk pace as he walked. These instant conferences were referred to as "walkie-talkies."

Journalist Bill Moyers, the President's press secretary, having dinner one night with the Johnson family, was asked to say grace. The President asked him to talk louder because he couldn't hear him. Moyers replied, "I wasn't talking to you, Mr. President."

To set a good example in his drive for economy, President Johnson turned out every light in the White House that wasn't absolutely necessary. He even turned out lights as he left rooms. Many staff members who left an office to go to the bathroom returned to find their offices dark. Others complained of bumping into each other along the dark corridors.

Richard M. Nixon (1969–1974)

Richard Nixon entered politics by answering an advertisement in a local California newspaper run by Republicans in the district. They needed a candidate to run for Congress, and Nixon was given the job. He won the Congressional seat in 1946.

First Lady Pat Nixon once worked as a Hollywood extra.

The first President for whom eighteen-year-olds could vote was Richard Nixon, in 1972.

The Twenty-sixth Amendment, changing the voting age from 21 to 18, was ratified in June 1971.

During the Eisenhower administration, Richard Nixon became the first Vice President to benefit from a 1955 increase in the Vice President's salary — from $30,000 to $35,000. When he took office as President in 1969, the presidential salary had just risen from $100,000 to $200,000.

During summer vacations while he was in high school, Richard Nixon worked at the Slippery Gulch Rodeo, in Arizona. He was the barker for the Wheel of Chance.

Nixon had a carriage accident at the age of two, which left him susceptible to motion sickness.

Nixon had to shave two or three times a day to appear clean-shaven during his political compaigns, because his beard grew in so fast.

Richard Nixon was named after King Richard the Lion-Hearted.

President Nixon's daughter Tricia was the first person to have an outdoor wedding at the

White House. She was married in the Rose Garden in June 1971.

One of Richard Nixon's favorite dishes was meat loaf.

Nixon was the first President to visit China while in office. He was also the first President to visit all fifty states.

When singer Pearl Bailey admired a gold chair in the White House East Room, President Nixon gave it to her.

On August 8, 1974, Richard Nixon resigned from the Presidency. Impeachment proceedings had already begun as a result of increasing evidence that the President had been involved in covering up a burglary by his campaign staff during the campaign of 1972. His was the only presidential resignation in American history.

Gerald R. Ford (1974–1977)

Gerald Ford was the only President who had once worked as a male model. He appeared in *Look* Magazine in an ad for a Vermont ski resort.

Susan Ford, the President's daughter, worked in the White House before her father did, selling White House guide books to tourists. One of her duties was to scurry behind a screen whenever a member of President Nixon's family passed by, to allow him or her maximum privacy.

In Grand Rapids, Michigan, Gerald Ford once won a trip to Washington in a contest run by a local movie theater as the "most popular high school senior."

President Ford's favorite lunch was cottage cheese smothered in catsup.

Gerald Ford did not know that he was adopted until he was sixteen. Ford was born Leslie Lynch King, Jr. When he was two, his parents divorced and his mother later married Gerald Rudolff Ford, who legally adopted the boy and gave him his own name. The secret was kept from him until his high school years, when his real father came up to him one day and announced the facts.

Playing football for the University of Michigan in his senior year, Gerald Ford was named Most Valuable Player. He received offers from the Green Bay Packers and the Detroit Lions, but declined them to accept a coaching job at Yale, where he later studied law.

Betty Ford, the President's wife, was originally Elizabeth Ann Bloomer. She had studied dancing with the famous Martha Graham Company.

Gerald Ford was able to get by on only four hours sleep a night.

One night Betty Ford heard the President talking in his sleep, saying, "Thank you, thank you, thank you." Later, he said he had been dreaming about being in a receiving line.

In his early days at the White House, Gerald Ford toasted his own English muffin for breakfast.

Betty and Gerald Ford's house in Alexandria, Virginia, bought before he was President, cost $34,000. After he left the White House the house sold for $137,000.

On the day of her wedding to Gerald Ford, he is reported to have shown up with one brown shoe and one black.

Another night President Ford took his golden retriever for a walk on the South Lawn and locked himself out. The President found all the entrances locked and figured he'd have to spend the rest of the night in an entrance hall in bathrobe and slippers, but a guard discovered him and let him in.

Gerald Ford was the first Vice President to be appointed by a President under the Twenty-fifth Amendment.

Within the space of seventeen days in 1975, two attempts were made on President Ford's life.

On his first day out of office, former President Gerald Ford played in a golf tournament in California.

Jimmy Carter (1977–)

Jimmy Carter, the first Deep Southerner elected President since the Civil War, was a peanut farmer in Plains, Georgia, before his election. As part of the Inauguration Day parade, a giant air-filled peanut was floated down Pennsylvania Avenue.

President Carter's brother, Billy, is allergic to peanuts.

Invitations to the Carter inauguration were printed on recycled paper. Some 300,000 were sent to those who had helped in the campaign, mainly as souvenirs, but three quarters of those who received invitations showed up. One group, from Carter's hometown of Plains, Georgia, hired its own train, the "Peanut Special," and ate 275 pounds of peanuts on their way to Washington.

President Carter was the first Chief Executive to walk from the Capitol to the White House — a distance of about a mile and a half — after his inauguration.

Carter began, at the age of twelve, to write letters to people who might recommend him as a candidate for the U. S. Naval Academy at Annapolis. Afraid that his flat feet would eliminate him from Annapolis consideration, he stood on Coke bottles and rolled back and forth to strengthen his arches.

As a young naval officer, Jimmy Carter suffered from seasickness. When he had to stand watch, he carried a bucket along.

At the dinner table, the President's daughter sometimes recited the blessing with the help of her toy toaster which popped up Bible verses.

Jimmy Carter was the first President to run a TV talk show. Called "Ask Mr. Carter," it was on for two hours, during which time viewers called in with questions or advice for the President. Nine million people made phone calls; forty-two of them actually got through.

For a single Jimmy Carter reception, the White House pastry chef baked 18,000 cookies.

In General

Three Presidents were lefthanded: Garfield, Truman, and Ford.

The official salute to the President is twenty-one guns with four ruffles and flourishes. The Vice President receives nineteen guns with four ruffles and flourishes.

Secret Service men are not responsible to or answerable to the President. The White House Secret Service boss can order a President not to go somewhere and he must obey.

Four Presidents in a row, Jefferson, Madison, Monroe, and John Quincy Adams, were former Secretaries of State.

John F. Kennedy, the youngest man ever elected to the Presidency, took over the office from the oldest man to serve as President, Dwight D. Eisenhower.

Most Presidents were Episcopalian. Thomas Jefferson, Abraham Lincoln, and Andrew Johnson had no official religion.

Three Presidents died on the Fourth of July: John Adams, Jefferson, and Monroe. One President, Calvin Coolidge, was born on that day.

Only two Presidents lived past their ninetieth birthdays: John Adams and Herbert Hoover.

Two Presidents received Nobel Peace Prizes: Theodore Roosevelt and Woodrow Wilson.

Two unrelated Presidents were born within twelve miles of each other: William Henry Harrison, the ninth President, and John Tyler, the tenth President, who were born in Charles City County, Virginia.

In more than one third of the presidential elections, the President of the United States has been elected without receiving a majority of the popular vote.

The White House has 132 rooms, including a barbershop, a movie theater, a swimming pool, offices for a physician and a dentist, a bomb shelter, and a solarium. There are 27 bathrooms, plus 12 in the office wings.

George Washington was called the "Father of His Country." James Madison was called the "Father of the Constitution." Both men were childless.

When workmen in 1902 tore down White House walls, they found the names of workmen who had repaired the White House in 1814.

The White House, official home of the President of the United States, is Reservation Number 1 of the National Capital Parks, National Park Service, Department of the Interior.

Neither the Franklin D. Roosevelts nor the Hoovers would sit at a table set for thirteen guests.

About 180 children have lived in the White House, the first being the four-year-old granddaughter of John Adams. Five Presidents lived in a childless White House: Polk, Pierce, Buchanan, McKinley, and Harding.

Twice the United States has had three Presidents in one year: Van Buren, William Henry Harrison, and Tyler in 1841, and Hayes, Garfield, and Arthur in 1881.

Two Presidents could take shorthand: James Madison and Woodrow Wilson.

No President of the United States was born in June.

About a third of the Presidents had more than eight sisters and brothers.

No President was an only child.

Until the 1850s, American Indian chiefs used to come to Washington to negotiate with Presidents and were treated as foreign diplomats.

The first two presidential candidates who debated on TV — Richard M. Nixon and John F. Kennedy — became President. Kennedy won the election following the debate, but Nixon was elected eight years later.

In order to pay the salaries of the first President and members of Congress, the Government of the United States had to borrow money. The Bank of New York and the Bank of North America made the loan.

At the First Constitutional Convention, in 1787, it was proposed that the President hold office for seven years.

Protocol at the White House demands that the President be served first at meals, that he get into a car first, and that when he enters a room, everyone stands. No one is allowed to leave the table or the room before he does.

The John Adams family hauled water to the White House from springs a mile and a half away. Jefferson installed a cistern in the attic, with wooden pipes leading through the floors. Van Buren added a reservoir in the basement which could be pumped for kitchen and bath use. It was not until the mid-1800s that the President could take a bath in a bathtub.

More Presidents were born in the month of October than in any other month.

Two Presidents had the same birthday, November 2: Polk and Harding.

Harvard University was attended by more Presidents than any other college.

More Presidents had the name James (Madison, Monroe, Polk, Buchanan, Garfield, Carter) than any other first name.

No two Presidents in succession died in office.

No President was born on the third of the month.

The President of the United States is entitled, in addition to salary, expenses for travel and entertainment and, free of charge, living accommodations at the White House; a fleet of automobiles for his use; a couple of dozen Secret Service men to guard him and his family; a yacht; an airplane; horses; a physician; a library; the use of an Army or Navy hospital; a police force to guard the White House estate; domestic servants; and an armor-plated Pullman car with bullet-proof windows.

A former President is entitled to a $60,000 annual pension, free mailing privileges, use of Government planes, office space, Secret Service protection, and an allowance of $90,000 for office help.

There are more items about Franklin D. Roosevelt in this book than about any other President.